M000318013

EVERYTHING HERE

Sibling Rivalry Press, LLC
PO Box 26147
Little Rock, AR 72221

info@siblingrivalrypress.com

www.siblingrivalrypress.com

ISBN: 978-1-943977-62-8

By special invitation, this title is housed in the Rare Book and Special Collections Vault of the Library of Congress.

First Sibling Rivalry Press Edition, September 2019

Four poems ("Crush;" "The Way It Expands;" "Peninsula with Guidebook;" and "Pancakes") appear in the following journal: *Hummingbird: Magazine of the Short Poem*, Vol. XIX, No. 1 (2019).

EVERYTHING HERE

BILLIE SWIFT

SIBLING RIVALRY PRESS
DISTURB/ENRAPTURE
Little Rock, Arkansas

Contents

Needle

Freedom is a needle
or mother
is a mop.

A stadium is a whirr
of flying fish.

This isn't what I meant:
Your evening
is a blackberry fist.

Cloud this light home
or ring my night done.

Freedom is a needle or
mother is a mop,
a stadium, a whirr
of flying fish.

Crush

Where the water pools in the gravel path
I step aside. Or

I'm splayed thumb-sized, a dark pink bud
open to a dozen dark pink butterflies
all smaller than a robin's eye. Or

I'm the grey of loose gravel, crushed
and sounding like *Crush. Crush.*

Once I was even the wind
and the sun kept trying to shine,
shining, shine like a dream
that won't stop hiding.

Peninsula with Guidebook

In the story with lava the girl

jumped having been pursued

this being where she landed

hands palm down in the molten

earth it sounds even worse

when you use the word escaped.

Laws of Motion

There's a window
with real things through it.
Some trees. A moon.
The neighbor's roof. There are cats
two of them, asleep
or yawning. The dog
breathes once every two seconds.
My fingernails are dirty.
There are corners
to sweep.

There's a moon
in the corner. Two cats
sleep on it. The neighbor
sweeps the trees. The windows
yawn. They are dirty. The dog
breathes fingers through the roof
of his nails. Things are real
once every two seconds.

My breath is a dirty roof.
Things yawn once every
two seconds. The moon
is cornered. A window
fingers the neighbor's

trees. Cat sweeps
dog. Dog nails
sleep. Sleep
sweeps through.

Metamorphoses

We keep warm in our monkey suits
we are spiders and dragons

a parrot's beak
a lion's mane

until we learn to purr
cup our buds in coconuts and shells
grow into nurses and maids

we save the soldiers coming home with our bare knees
we are historic and historical
hysterical
or Joan of Arc

one of us is even a line from Ulysses
or a word

then one of us is a word

the perfect word
we coo and we coo

Pancakes

Sturdy clouds settle
down the lawn's slow back

Each blink is a bruise

Heavy trucks push
their sounds through

rattling last night's plates

The children wake
wanting

Still Life

Look straight watch the cat
        aside from pieces
watch me watch the dog
        here and there when
watching me watch the light
        he'll need me
changing change the room
        to pick him up
room full of shadows
        or drop him off
shadows full of room
        then he'll be
shadows of the room
        gone and I'll
watch the shadows
        re-live my life
creep around bend around
        and I'll be home
sweep the room watch
        in my chair
the shadows reach around
        my blanket barely
to clear the air watch
        long enough to cover
the changing light

            my toes the tea
stretch fade twist
            not cool enough to drink
and shrink watch
            the room will be quiet
the shadows wind
            my book will be open
the light anything but
            my book will rest
the stillness
            on my legs calling
of this room this
            in several tongues
is not what we meant
            at once I realize
we didn't know
            it's the phone and it's time
the choice we made
            to go what if this
unmakes our bed of down
            is everything the excitement
and many pillows
            of a lifetime the phone
we agreed to life
            ringing for the last time
we agreed on making
            the last time I kick off
life after we passed

the blanket and spill
the no going back
     my tea while
I told myself
     stumbling over the dog
it felt good to be
     the last time I'll
full up with a life
     ask myself why
I'll never have
     the rush where's the fire?

Before/After

I'm in the passenger seat picking cat hair
from my black wool sweater.

In a dark room we search the wall
for a light.

In the morning
I watch the sun spread open the clouds.

On the way back the trees are everywhere.

You to Myself

Through these minor refusals
we hold our mutual
eternities, our shared bits of air.

I listen at how thoroughly
you chew your small squares of irrelevance.

What we mean makes sense, which is why
I never explain you to myself.

It's what the tongue must do
to keep the other still.

Festiva Maxima

I keep walking in
to find the flower smaller, a pile of petals
on the table, but always still—

never less than what it is.

The wait is long. I stay
still, wanting to be that important.

Landscape Kitchen Table

Steller's jay in the tree outside,
top branch. He's pretty.

> In the middle of the afternoon
> the edges are soft and lack a name
> for what goes in the middle.

There's a crow just came. Flew in
right below.

> In the middle of a thought
> clarity of purpose shines
> like a reflective surface.

The jay retreats for a bit, an awkward
flap of wings.

> In the middle of the table
> a tulip's stem round and smooth bends
> toward a miraculous bolt of color.

He's back. The crow remains.
Now the jay is screaming.

> The tulip is red. What does
> that mean?

Now he's not.

Gave to Feed

The owls asleep in trees

    too high for milk drunk

        eyes to climb or to be quiet

    through skies of branches

dripping shadows while stars

    below keep spinning

        sending windows through

    the glass and ringing spoons

the sound of someone calling

    and can't find my name

        determined that we raise

    our voices maybe it's under

the couch with me.

The Sincerity of These Questions
Troubles My Sleep

Compare this to a bird.
The bird will be like a pencil
shading, coloring. The bird will be
a blue colored pencil. The time
will be day.

Compare this to black.
The black will be a warm
rug. I will stare into the soft heat
before I hit it with my face
and wake up.

Compare this to a subtle
hint of red. The hint of red
will be the shadow that moves
with my body until the shadow is
my body and I wake up.

Compare this to flight.
The flight will be my hand
pushing through the dark,
the feel of nothing
against my palm.

Memory of a Sound

How heavy it was that first night
    and more urgent

The way I remember it
    as the physical sensation
    of milk

How long it lasted
    as an ache in my arms

Making it stop

What I offered the gods

The Way It Expands

The homemaker finds a hair in the dough.
She asks, *What is this?* The hair turns grey.
Grey as the veining in her Carrara marble
countertops. The woman's face hardens.
The hair sees her for the first time, this
forgotten statue in the park. But the woman
smiles. A crematorium blaze lightens her
face. She says, *Hair, of course I still love you.*
Of course you can stay. Then, as though she
were a dog, she eats it, and all the dough,
her eyes widening as the final lumps bulge
her throat. Raw dough will kill a dog. The
way it expands, maybe—or how hunger has
nothing to do with it.

How to Take Pity

With a side of gin

Cut with ice

Unwillingly

In both hands

Steadily

By the shoulders and shaken

Until all the tears fall out

On the kitchen counter

With a slice of lemon

From behind

Like you mean it

When We Fight We Fight Dirty

What's yellow above me. The leaves

    are yellow. The sky is blue. The leaves

are green. The sky is blue. The leaves

    are yellow & green. The sky is blue.

The leaves are orange & red. The sky

    is blue. The leaves are yellow & green

red & brown. The sky is blue

    & free of any white cloud, grey bird, shiny

plane or flapping sign, smoke trail

    or factory churn, yellow beak or

V formation, wing curve, blade pulse

    or the loud smoke of war & how much

we get carried away & what for.

Bespoke a Little Perspective

5:45
Today is a box. A box is a day. A day
is a box of to.

6:30
The rise and fall of moth dust
inside limbs of light.

9:45
Everything here—each sound—and all
the sounds that aren't almost.

10:15
The hum of cool and clock. The click
of dog.

12:24
This hold of glass. A smudge
the shape of lips.

1:30
Falling yellow leaves make time
from branch to ground without
my explication.

3:30
Heads bent around a beetle
on its back. Legs
thin and broken into joints
curling for the air.
This beetle takes my stare!

10:30
Careless wonder wanders in. A doll's
shoe, stickers
on the wall.

Evening Into Night

A tree trunk outside the window. The window's
glass. The houseplant on the windowsill.

      Sirens distract from nothing.

The tree is there, but I can't see it now. The glass
in the window is looking at me. The houseplant
stays quiet.

      I'm not hungry. My fingers are full of pen.

The room behind me is outside the window.
I drink tea without mentioning my thirst.

      The glass is room-shaped.

About the Poet

Billie Swift lives in Seattle, Washington, where she is the owner and operator of Open Books: A Poem Emporium. She received an MFA in poetry from the Rainier Writing Workshop at Pacific Lutheran University.

About the Press

Sibling Rivalry Press is an independent press based in Little Rock, Arkansas. It is a sponsored project of Fractured Atlas, a nonprofit arts service organization. Contributions to support the operations of Sibling Rivalry Press are tax-deductible to the extent permitted by law, and your donations will directly assist in the publication of work that disturbs and enraptures. To contribute to the publication of more books like this one, please visit our website and click *donate*.

Sibling Rivalry Press gratefully acknowledges the following donors, without whom this book would not be possible:

Tony Taylor
Mollie Lacy
Karline Tierney
Maureen Seaton
Travis Lau
Michael Broder & Indolent Books
Robert Petersen
Jennifer Armour
Alana Smoot
Paul Romero
Julie R. Enszer
Clayton Blackstock
Tess Wilmans-Higgins & Jeff Higgins
Sarah Browning
Tina Bradley
Kai Coggin
Queer Arts Arkansas
Jim Cory
Craig Cotter
Hugh Tipping
Mark Ward

Russell Bunge
Joe Pan & Brooklyn Arts Press
Carl Lavigne
Karen Hayes
J. Andrew Goodman
Diane Greene
W. Stephen Breedlove
Ed Madden
Rob Jacques
Erik Schuckers
Sugar le Fae
John Bateman
Elizabeth Ahl
Risa Denenberg
Ron Mohring & Seven Kitchens Press
Guy Choate & Argenta Reading Series
Guy Traiber
Don Cellini
John Bateman
Gustavo Hernandez
Anonymous (12)

CPSIA information can be obtained
at www.ICGtesting.com
Printed in the USA
LVHW030033030120
642350LV00007B/1189/P

9 781943 977628